Handbook for
English Concertina

by
Roger
Watson

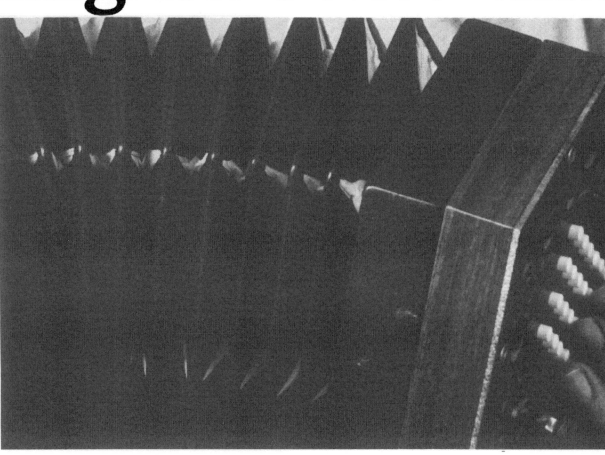

EXCLUSIVELY DISTRIBUTED BY

HAL•LEONARD®

Published by
Hal Leonard

Exclusive Distributors:
Hal Leonard
7777 West Bluemound Road,
Milwaukee, WI 53213
Email: info@halleonard.com

Hal Leonard Europe Limited
42 Wigmore Street Maryleborne,
London, WIU 2 RY
Email: info@halleonardeurope.com

Hal Leonard Australia Pty. Ltd.
4 Lentara Court Cheltenham,
Victoria, 9132 Australia
Email: info@halleonard.com.au

Order No. AM28317
ISBN 0 86001 851 2
This book © Copyright 1981 by Hal Leonard

Cover Design Cleaver Landor
Book Design Cleaver Landor
Photography Andrew kimm

Printed in EU.
www.halleonard.com

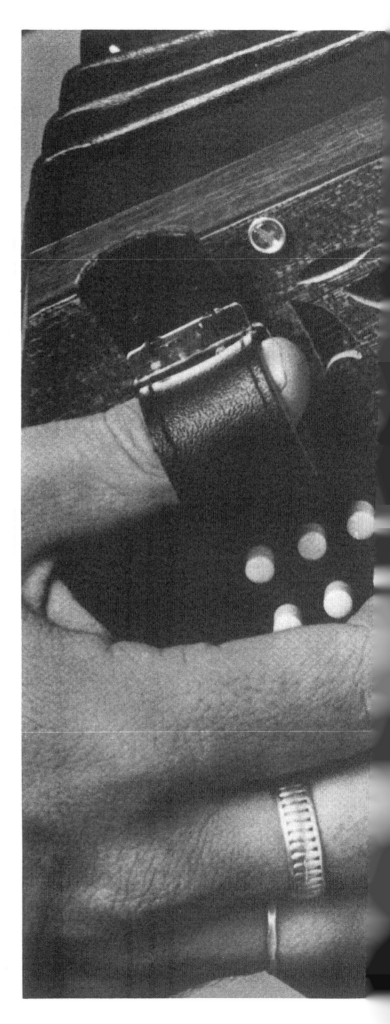

Contents

The Concertina and the Folk Music Revival

The English Concertina

The concertina belongs to the family of 'free reed' instruments, that is, instruments which make their sound by the passage of air vibrating metal reeds. Other instruments of this type are the harmonica, accordion, melodeon and harmonium.

The English concertina was invented in 1829 by Sir Charles Wheatstone, who registered a patent on the instrument. Classical pieces were written for it, and its large and fully chromatic range makes it capable of playing music written for such instruments as the violin, clarinet and oboe. But its tone has never appealed greatly to those involved in orchestral music. Instead, Wheatstone's invention, along with its close cousin, the Anglo-Chromatic concertina, became largely an instrument for 'popular' musicians.

The distinctive bellows action of the 'squeeze-box' has made the term 'concertina' almost universally known, to the extent that many do not take it seriously as an instrument. Yet, its versatility and portability led to its great popularity in the later 19th and in the 20th centuries. Travelling musicians and sailors found its compact size a great advantage; the Salvation Army made good use of its strident tone; concertina bands were popular in many towns particularly in the North; music hall performers demonstrated the extent of virtuosity which could be reached on the concertina. But the greatest and most long-lasting popularity of the instrument has been among singers and players of folk music.

There are two basic types of concertina. First, Wheatstone's English system, which plays the same note whether the bellows are pushed or pulled. It is fully chromatic, that is, it has all the sharps and flats necessary to play in all keys. An English concertina is recognizable by having four parallel straight rows of buttons on each end, thumb straps and little finger slides. Some English concertinas have wrist straps as well. The buttons for playing

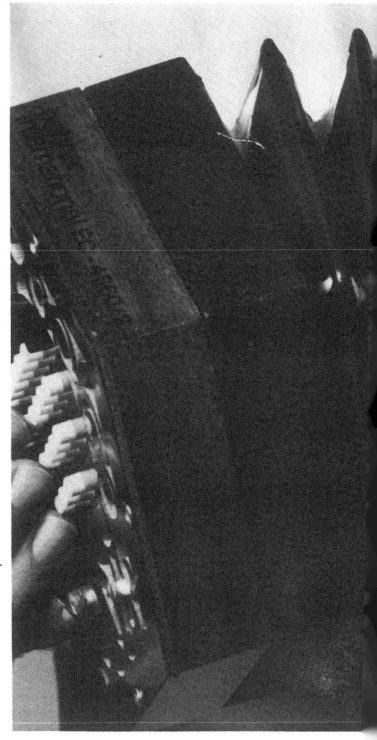

the lower notes are situated on the part of each end which is closer to the body when the instrument is held in the normal playing position. Notable makers of the English system were Wheatstone himself, Lachenal (an employee of Wheatstone who later formed an independent company), Jones and Crabbe. The firm of Crabbe are still producing a small number of instruments, and the Wheatstone company name has recently been revived, although production is, as yet, very small. Second, there is the Anglo-chromatic concertina ('Anglo' for short), which, like the harmonica and melodeon, also of Germanic origin, plays different notes when blown and sucked (that is, when the bellows are squeezed

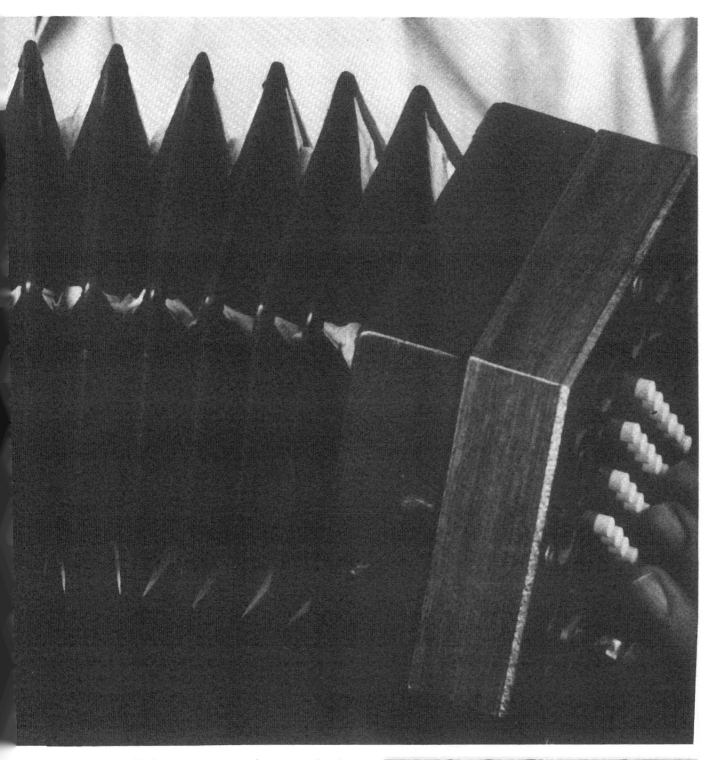

together or pulled apart). An Anglo concertina has wrist straps, and at least two rows of buttons arranged in an arc forward of straps. It has an air release button, usually correctly positioned for the right thumb. To be fully chromatic, an Anglo has to have a large number of buttons (with 30 or more, a number of keys are possible) as well as more variation within the basic keys of the two main rows. The lower notes are played by the buttons on the left hand side, and the higher ones by those on the right. Wheatstone, Lachenal, and Jeffries were the main producers of Anglos in the past, and Crabbe & Co., and Colin Dipper still produce them in small numbers today.

There is a third type of concertina, known as a 'Duet', for which there are various fingering systems, all attempting to combine the advantages of both main types - bass on the left, treble on the right; fully chromatic and the same note, push or pull. They have wrist straps like Anglos, and on some, key arrangement makes them look, at first glance, like an Anglo with a large number of buttons. But the 'acid test' is that only an Anglo has two different notes on one button.

Among folk players, those who favour the English system, and those who favour the Anglo are about equal in number. The Anglo, with its restriction on keys is not as popular for accompanying songs, although there are those who use it to great effect, notably John Kirkpatrick and the Rev. Kenneth Loveless. The inherent rhythm in the bellows action of the Anglo makes it an ideal instrument to play for ritual or social dance, and the legendary names in this field are the late William Kimber and Scan

with the instrument, while instilling it with a seemingly natural sense of rhythm, usually identifiable with the Anglo. Many Irish players use the Anglo for melody without accompaniment and their skill lies in the ability to control the bellows during fast and complex passages so that the Anglo displays the kind of fluid legato quality associated with the English. This smoothness, the ability to play chords in any key, and the soft tone of the English concertina, make it an ideal instrument for the accompaniment of songs. In the early days of the folk song revival, Alf Edwards' accompaniments of A.L. Lloyd, and Peggy Seeger's of Ewan MacColl set a pattern which influenced many followers, and singers such as Louis Killen and Tony Rose have developed styles of self-accompaniment on the instrument.

All this has added up to a great deal of interest in concertinas. Instruments which only a decade or so ago would have been thrown out with the rubbish are now changing hands for very large sums of money. This makes it difficult for the complete beginner to find an instrument which is both inexpensive and in good pitch and reliable condition. At the height of their production, both Wheatstone and Lachenal produced inexpensive 'tutor' models with coloured buttons, some stamped with the name of the note. Their tone was not as good as their more sophisticated counterparts but they were more than acceptable, and gave encouragement to the learner to keep practising and eventually progress to a better instrument. There are still a number of these in existence, but most

Tester, both of whom exerted a considerable influence on those who were lucky enough to hear them. The English concertina is not unknown among players for ritual dance, and it is widely used in social dance bands, largely, though not exclusively, as a purely melodic instrument to replace or complement the fiddle. Alistair Anderson of Newcastle has reached a very high degree of virtuosity in this area showing an ability to exploit fully the flowing quality of notes usually associated

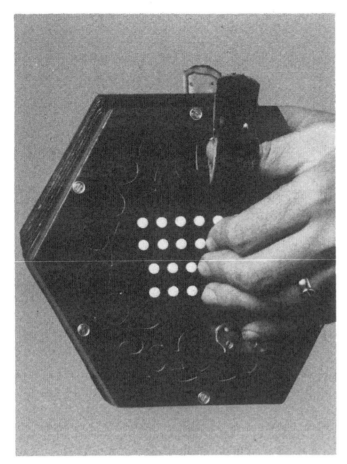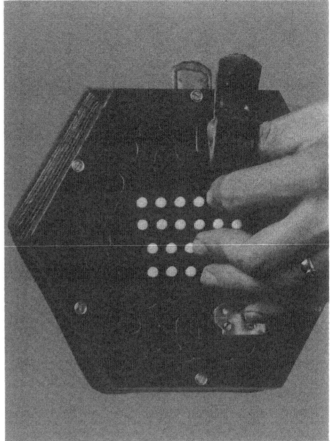

are now either quite difficult to find at a reasonable price, or badly in need of attention; and spare parts are difficult to obtain. The new Hohner concertinas are designed also to appeal to the learner. This handbook and fingering chart replace the old coloured and stamped buttons. But the instrument, although not outstanding is certainly adequate, and it is inexpensive and easy to service. It is good news for the beginner that a company with the experience of M.Hohner Ltd., is taking more than a passing interest in the instrument. Such interest is in itself a significant development in the history of the concertina.

Your Hohner English Concertina (treble or tenor) has 48 playing buttons (the black one is an air release button). Some concertinas have more buttons than this, but on the English system, whatever the number, they are arranged in the same way: four parallel straight rows between the thumb strap and the little finger rest. Each button operates a lever to lift a pad, so that opening or closing the bellows causes a passage of air to make the reed under that pad vibrate.

The system is different from the arrangement of notes on any other instrument, so whatever else you play, forget it.

Put your thumbs in the thumb straps and your little fingers in the slides. The ends of your little fingers should butt against the curved ends of the slides.

Adjust the thumb straps so that they fit snugly but not too tightly over the fleshy part of the thumb, covering the lower part of the nail but not the knuckle. This should give support and flexibility. Try as soon as possible to support the instrument entirely with your thumbs and little fingers, and don't be tempted to rest it on the heel of your hand, as this will restrict control of the playing keys. Your little fingers will not be used to this kind of supporting role, and at first they will *ache*. Some players prefer a sitting position, taking some of the weight of the instrument on a knee.

On each hand, the first finger usually controls the *two* rows of buttons nearest to the thumb strap, the middle finger the next row, and the third finger the row nearest to the little finger support. (see illust.)

To simplify things, we'll use the notation **L1** for the first finger of the left hand (**L1x** when it's used on the row nearest the thumb strap) **L2** for the left middle finger, **L3** for the left third finger and similarly **R1**, **R1x**, **R2** and **R3**.

To get used to the fingering pattern, forget the rows nearest to the thumb strap and finger slides, and concentrate on the middle two rows. These give you all the notes for the key of C, like the white notes on a piano. The outside rows give you the sharps and flats (black notes on a piano) to make the other keys.

Fingering Chart

Holding Position, **English** Concertina

Left   Right

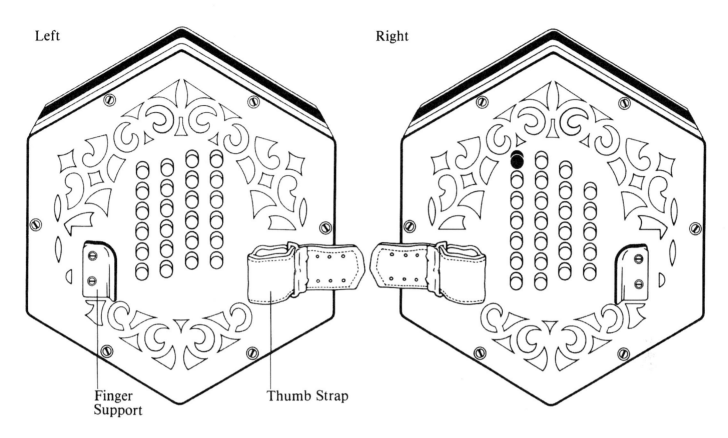

Finger
Support   Thumb Strap

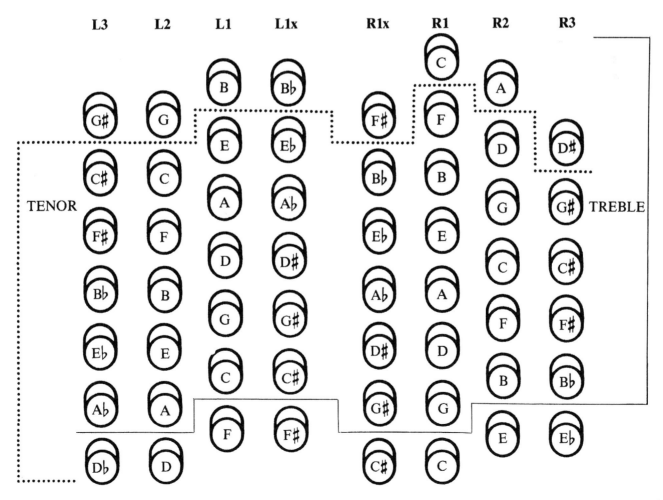

Diagrams Showing How to Play Scales

Press the button nearest to you on row **L2**, and pull the bellows gently but firmly from the closed position. Now transfer to **L1** with the appropriate finger. (Notice that this button is further forward than the one you were pressing with **L2**). If you then reach the same amount forward again with **L2** it should bring you to the next button on that row. Ignoring the actual notes you are making, continue this 'walking' action, alternating between **L1** and **L2**, right to the far end of those rows and back again, changing the direction of the bellows when necessary to keep an even flow of notes. Try the same with **R1** and **R2**.

Scale of C

To play the scale of C, start with the nearest button on row **L1** (second nearest, if you have the tenor model), then the second nearest on **R1** (third if you have the tenor model) and continue working forward, alternating sides and rows in the sequence **L1, R1, L2, R2**, and working back in the reverse of this sequence. You can come back further than your starting point (quite a way on the tenor) and still be playing notes in C as long as you stick to the middle rows. A glance at the fingering chart will tell you which keys actually play which notes. Keep in mind a smooth bellows action while you practise.

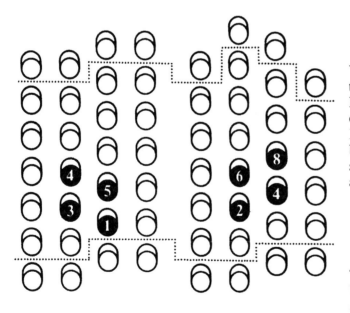

Playing scales is a good way of familiarising yourself with the basic system of the instrument. But you want to actually *play* something. Try the first of the selected tunes in this handbook. Don't panic if you've not read music before: the rows are marked above each note. If the notes are higher up the stave, it means that the buttons you press are further forward on the concertina.

Now do *that* without looking at your fingers!

In fact, it can never be too early to train yourself to find the next button, and even the starting button, without looking.

Scale of G

To play a scale of G in the middle range of the concertina, start one button further forward on **L1**, than you did to play the scale of C. Work your way forward, again in the sequence **L1, R1, L2, R2**.

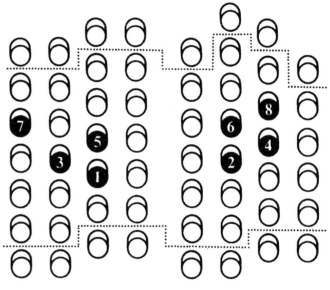

You will notice that your note on **L2** the second time is wrong: it's too low. It is in fact F instead of F sharp. And where's the F sharp? Right next to F on **L3**! So you still use the 'walking' action, but use **L3** on that occasion. In the same way, if you come back down the scale beyond the point where you started, the next note down on **R2** is again an F, and the F sharp you actually need is next to it on **R3**.

Scale of F

To play a scale in F, start on the second nearest button on **R2** (third nearest on the tenor model), and the sequence, going up the scale is as follows: **R2**(F), **L1**(G), **R1**(A), **L3**(B *flat*), **R2**(C), **L1**(D), **R1**(E), **L2**(F). Carry on, forwards on the concertina, up the scale, and you'll find that the next **R1** is wrong; the note you want is on **R1x** next to it.

And that is the beauty of it. Until you get into really obscure keys with frightening numbers of sharps and flats, whenever a note on the middle rows doesn't fit in with the sequence you want, the right one is next to it on the outside row.

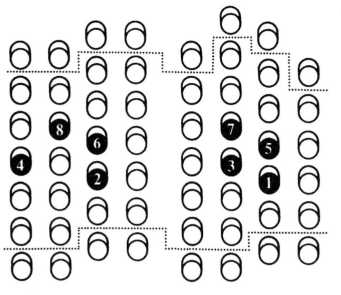

A look at the fingering chart will locate notes on which to start scales, and the tunes in the back give practice in the most popular keys for playing in with other instruments: G, D, C and F. If you get involved in a session with melodeon and fiddle players, the chances are you will be playing in G and D almost all the time. Also included, are tunes in E minor and B flat. No amount of practice from written music is anywhere near as valuable as working out the tunes you want to play by ear. Only in this way will you develop any individuality of style or repertoire.

When you're playing tunes or song melody lines, you can take advantage of one of the main features of the instrument: the ability to press one button in a sequence of notes marginally before lifting your finger from the previous one, thus giving a smooth transition between notes.

Hope you're still practising without looking at your fingers.

Chords

Tunes and melody lines are fine, but many of you will want to use the instrument to accompany singing in a rather fuller way, by using chords for all or part of the time. Chords on the English Concertina are relatively easy, and the easiest of all are two-finger chords. Any two buttons next to each other on the same side of the concertina and in the same key sequence will give notes that harmonise. For example, the button on **L1** which gives the starting note for the C scale, and the next button forward on **L2** give a chord, a very basic chord of C. The same button on **L1** will also harmonise with the one immediately forward of it, and to do this you can use a finger which would normally control another row; or you can cover two buttons with one finger, which is not so reliable.

Chord of C

To get a fuller chord of C, however, you can use both sides at once, either three or four fingers. Press the buttons mentioned above on **L1** and **L2**. Then, the nearest button on **R1** (second nearest on tenor model) and you have a three-finger chord of C. If you have a tenor, you add the nearest button on **R2** and make a four-finger chord. Keep the same relative finger position, and move each forward one button (you can add the fourth finger on the treble concertina now) and you have a chord of G. Another row forward, swapping **L2** for **L3** and **R2** for **R3** and you have a chord of D. Another row, and you have A. These are not the only C, G, D and A chords on the concertina, however. If you start with an F button on the right hand, that is, the second nearest on **R2** (third if you have the tenor) and add the next forward on **R1**, the nearest (second nearest on the tenor) on **L1** and **L2**, you have a four-finger chord of F. One button forward and you have another C chord. Forward again, and there's another G.

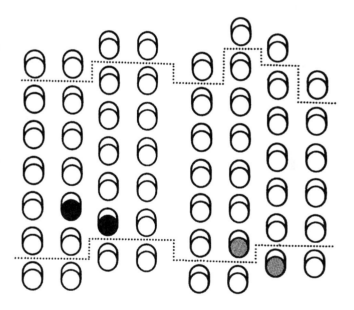

The notes in black on this diagram are the simple two finger chords described above. The shaded notes can be added to give a fuller chord.

The next couple of pages show the buttons on both sides, which can be used in any combination of two or more to make up chords. You can use these chords just like guitar chords to accompany songs, or between runs of melody or harmony, using whatever fingers you have spare to build an appropriate chord on the last note of a line. Some specimen song accompaniments are suggested at the back of this book; they are intended to give you ideas for accompaniments of your own.

Pattern of Chords

C (Add ● For C7)

B♭ (Add ● For B♭7)

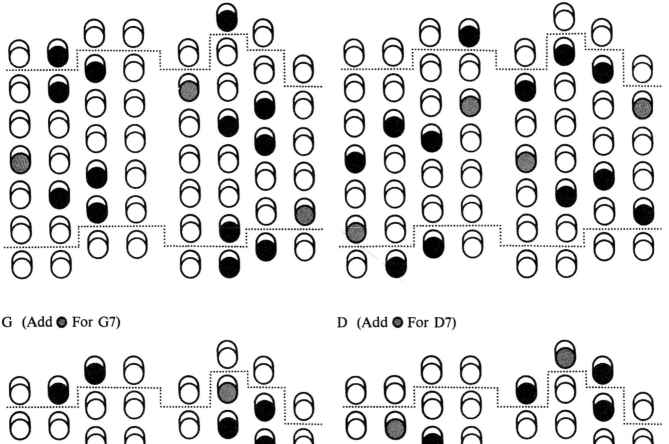

G (Add ● For G7)

D (Add ● For D7)

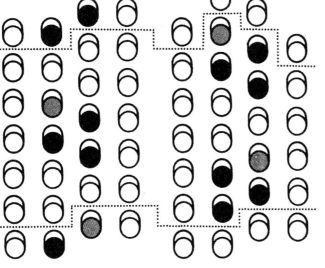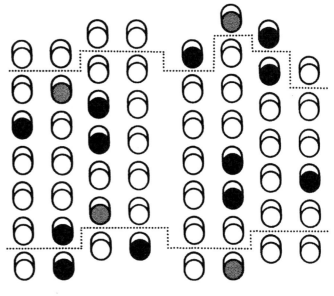

F (Add ● For F7)

A (Add ● For A7)

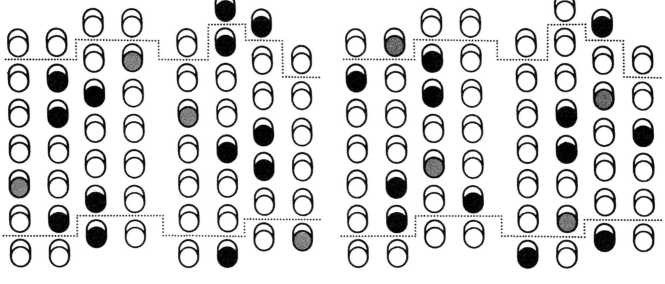

E♭ (Add ⬤ For E♭7)

D minor

A minor

G minor

E minor

B minor

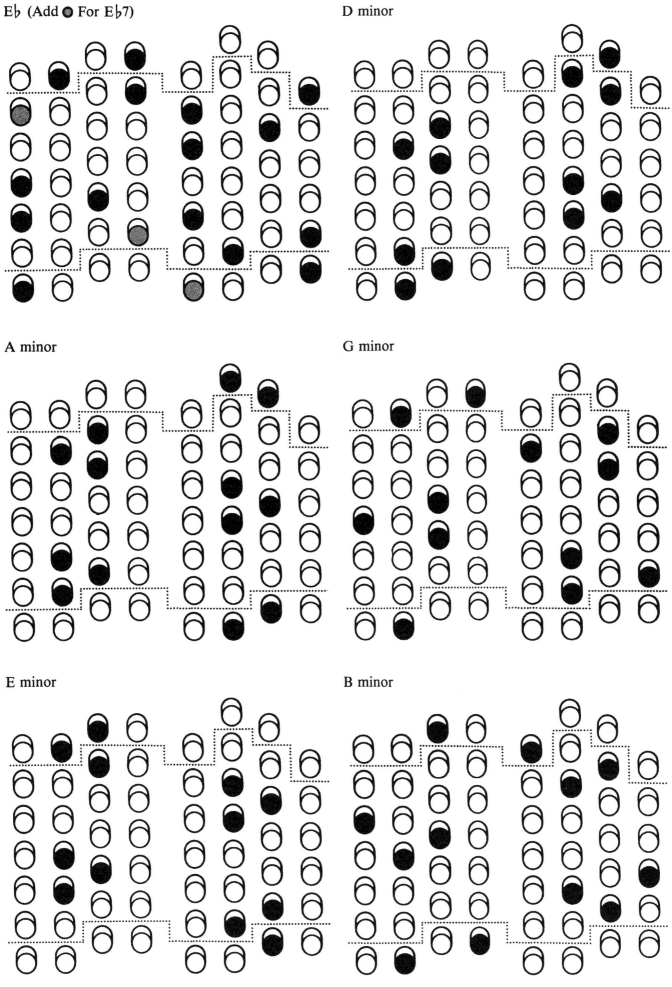

Selection of Tunes and song accompaniments

This selection of tunes and song accompaniments is intended to illustrate various principles which the player can use to build up his or her own repertoire. It is hoped that many of the inclusions will be familiar, so that those whose ability to read printed music is limited will at least have some idea of how the end-product should sound.

Most of the tunes are popular in folk festival musicians' sessions, either informal or arranged parts of most festivals. These sessions are an excellent place to practise tunes which you already know, and to learn new ones. The number of instruments is usually large enough for the occasional mistake by a learner to be masked, and the overall atmosphere is encouraging.

For those who envisage the concertina as part of a group line-up, the chords for guitar/banjo/piano are included. As mentioned in the text, these can be used in conjunction with the chord diagrams to develop a fuller concertina version of each tune. The accompaniment to Tune no. 12, 'Lord Franklin', gives some suggestions as to how this may be done.

Winster Gallop

Starts on C (first button on **L1**, or second on the tenor model). One of the most popular dance tunes. Practise each half separately and then put them together. The second half also starts on C, but an octave higher than the opening. It is a good idea to get your fingers used to the transition between the last note of the first part of this tune and the first note of the second part. The runs down the scale at the start of the second part give plenty of scope for overlapping adjacent notes.

The British Grenadiers

Starts on G: first button on **R1** (second on the tenor model). The first four bars are repeated. There are some faster passages and runs in this one, and a couple of occasions where two adjacent notes in the tune are on the same row, thus making it necessary for all the playing fingers to be off the keyboard for a brief moment. This is when you discover if you are really supporting the instrument by your thumbs and little fingers.

The Man in the Moon

Starts on D, second (third) button up on **R1**. This one is in the key of G and uses **R3** to give the necessary F sharp. Again the first part is repeated, to give you a chance to prove that getting it right first time wasn't a fluke. Try to get about two bars in one movement of the bellows; the change of bellows direction at the beginning of a bar will help to give rhythm to the waltz.

The Week Before Easter

In the key of F, but starts on C, the one that's on **L1**. It is a well-known song tune, and in this key uses **L3** for the necessary B flat. Filling in two finger chords at the end of lines by consultation with the chord chart should not be too difficult.

Here are the words to all the verses:

The week before Easter, the morn bright and clear,
The sun it shone brightly and keen blew the air,
I went to the forest to gather fine flowers,
But the forest won't yield me no roses.

The roses are red my love, the leaves they are green,
The bushes and briars are fair to be seen,
The small birds are whistling and changing their notes,
All among the wild flowers in the forest.

The first time I saw my love to the church go,
With the bridegroom and bridesmaids she made a fine show,
And I followed on with a heart full of woe,
For I had not the fortune to wed her.

The parson that married them, so loud did he cry,
'All you that forbid it, I would have you draw nigh'.
And I thought to myself, 'I've a good reason why',
But I had not the heart to forbid it.

And when that I saw my love sit down to dine,
I sat down beside her and poured out the wine,
And I drank to the lassie that should have been mine,
Though now she was wed to another.

The men of yon forest, they ask it of me,
How many strawberries grow in the salt sea?
And I answer them back with a tear in my eye,
How many ships sail in the forest?

Go dig me a grave, dig it long, wide and deep,
And cover it over with flowers so sweet,
And I will turn in there and have a long sleep,
Then maybe in time I'll forget her.

The Dorset Four-Hand Reel

Another popular dance tune in the key of G, using the higher F sharp on row **L3**. When you've practised this one, go back to 'Winter Gallop', and try playing that in G, the key in which it is more usually played. The transposition is easy: just start one button further forward on the same row, and use the **L3** button where **L2** doesn't fit. Otherwise the fingering pattern is exactly the same. Try it with 'The British Grenadiers' as well; there you will have to use the F sharp on **R3** which was used in 'Man in the Moon'.

Landlord Fill the Flowing Bowl

Another one in F, exploring some of the lower notes in that key. Also included are some suggestions for harmonising parts of the melody using simple two finger chords. Practise the melody straight for the first few times, then add the extra finger. Be careful that you still hit the melody note when you do! Often, a row will be used for melody one beat and harmony the next.

Landlord, fill the flowing bowl, until it doth run over(x2)
For tonight we'll be merry, merry be,(x3)
Tomorrow we'll be sober.

The man who drinks pure water clear and goes to bed quite sober(x2)
Fades as the leaves will fall(x3)
And dies off in October.

The man who drinks strong ale and beer and goes to bed quite mellow(x2)
Lives as he ought to live (x3)
And dies a jolly good fellow.

Here's to the girl who steals a kiss and runs to tell her mother(x2)
She's a very foolish thing(x3)
She'll never get another.

Here's to the girl who steals a kiss and comes back for another(x2)
She's a boon to all mankind(x3)
For soon she'll be a mother.

Planxty Irwin

A beautiful melody from the Irish harper
O'Carolan. In the key of D, starting high up on **L1**
(check with the fingering chart if necessary) this one
uses the two F sharps we've already encountered,
on **R3** and **L3** and also a C sharp on **R3** and one on
L1x. Try to play **L1x** by moving that finger only

out of position and still keeping **L2** and **L3** covering
their respective rows. Don't take your little finger
out of the slide when you move your first finger
across. Feel for it, but don't look.

John Barleycorn

There are two ways of thinking about minor keys when playing the English concertina: they can be considered relative to the major key of the same name, but with a slightly different progression up the scale, or relative to the major key that has the same key signature. The one sharp of E minor is the same as that in G major, and the scale and fingering patterns are just the same, but starting at a different point in the scale. In the same way, A minor is the same as C, D minor is the same as F, and so on. Actually, 'John Barleycorn' isn't really in E minor at all but in the transposed Dorian mode here based on E, but the only note of difference between the two doesn't occur in the tune. Many traditional songs have modal tunes, not fitting strictly into either major or minor keys, and the style of chord accompaniment used with them has been a matter for much discussion, and must be left to individual taste. The chords printed are therefore only a suggestion.

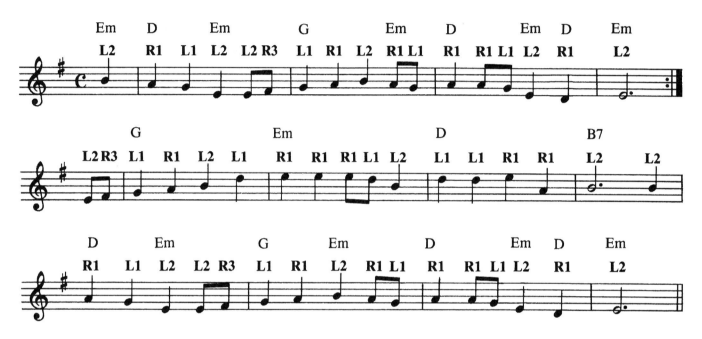

There were three men came out of the west, their fortune for to try
And these three men made a solemn vow, John Barleycorn should die
They ploughed, they sowed, they harrowed him in,
Threw clods upon his head, and these three men made a solemn vow,
John Barleycorn was dead.

They let him lie for a very long time and the rain from heaven did fall
Then little Sir John sprung up his head and so amazed them all.
They let him lie till Midsummer,
Till he looked both pale and wan,
Then little Sir John he growed a long beard, and so became a man.

They hired men with the scythes so sharp to cut him off at the knee
They rolled him and tied him by the waist and served him barbarously
They hired men with crabtree sticks,
To thrash him skin from bone,
But the miller he served him worse than that, for he ground him between two stones.

Here's little Sir John in the nut brown bowl, and Brandy in a glass,
But little Sir John in the nut brown bowl proved the strongest man at last.
For the huntsman he can't follow the fox, nor so loudly blow his horn.
And the tinker he can't mend kettles and pots, without a little John Barleycorn.

A fuller text to a similar tune can be found in the Penguin Book of English Folksongs.

Adieu, Sweet Lovely Nancy

Another well-known song, from the Copper family of Sussex. In the key of B flat, it uses a B flat note on **R3**, a higher one on **L3** and an E flat on **L3** as well. As with the tune 'Landlord Fill the Flowing Bowl', some harmonic phrases are suggested using two-finger chords, and three-finger ones at the end of lines.

Here's adieu, sweet lovely Nancy, ten thousand times adieu.
I'm bound across the ocean wide, to seek for something new.
Come change your ring with me, dear girl, come change your ring with me,
That it might be a token of true love, when I am on the sea.

When I'm far across the ocean, you will know not where I am.
Kind letters I will write to you from every foreign land.
The secrets of my heart, dear girl, and the best of my good will,
For let my body be where it might, my heart will be with you still.

There's a heavy storm arising, see how it gathers round,
While we poor souls on the ocean wide are piping for the ground.
There is nothing to protect us, love, or keep us from the cold,
On the ocean wide, where we must bide, like jolly seamen bold.

There are tinkers, tailors, shoemakers lie snoring fast asleep,
While we poor souls on the ocean wide are ploughing up the deep.
Our officers commanded us, and them we must obey,
Expecting every moment for to get cast away.

And when the wars are over, there'll be peace on every shore,
We'll return to our wives and our families, and the girls that we adore,
We'll call for liquor merrily, and spend our money free.
And when our money it is all spent, we'll boldly go to sea.

21

Jockey to the Fair

Two jig rhythm tunes which can be played at a slightly faster pace. But be careful not to rush them too early until the fingering pattern is familiar. The rhythm can be accentuated by a careful control of the bellows; but take care not to get them too wide or too close, or the faster passages on high notes in 'Off She Goes' will be difficult. 'Jockey to the Fair' is in G, but contains a C sharp on **R3** on one occasion; in all other places it's a straight C on **R2**.

Off She Goes

22

Lord Franklin

An example of how the concertina can be used to accompany a ballad without actually playing the tune, but using chords, snatches of melody or harmony and harmonic runs.

You can try adapting these principles to the other songs in the book, in consultation with the chord chart, perhaps. Another useful practice might be to work out the melody without the row notation; if you haven't read music before, look at the other tunes in F (one flat at the beginning of each line) and see what buttons were used for notes in the same places on the stave.

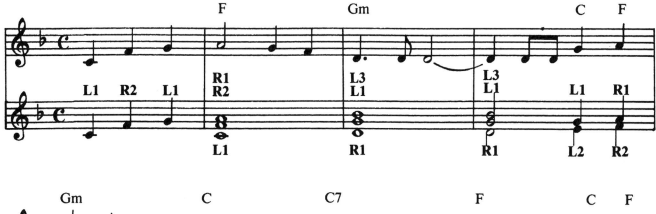

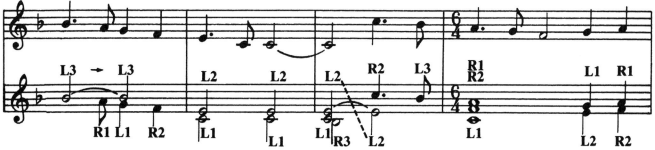

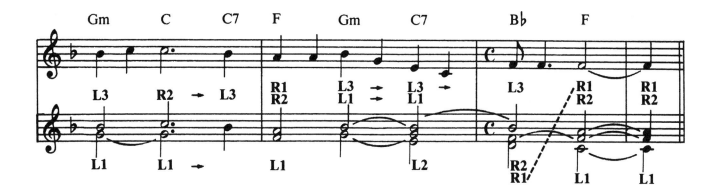

'Twas homeward bound, one night on the deep,
Swinging in my hammock I fell asleep,
I dreamed a dream, and I thought it true,
Concerning Franklin and his gallant crew.

With a hundred seamen, he sailed away,
To the frozen ocean in the month of May
To find that passage around the Pole
Where we poor sailors do sometimes go.

Through cruel hardships his men did go,
His ship on mountains of ice was blown,
Where the Eskimo, in his skin canoe
Was the only one that ever came through.

In Baffin's Bay, where the whalefish blow,
The fate of Franklin no man do know,
The fate of Franklin, no man can tell,
Lord Franklin along with his sailors do dwell.

And now my burden, it gives me pain,
For my long-lost Franklin, I would cross the main,
Ten thousand pounds would I freely give,
To know on earth that my Franklin lives.

Care and Maintenance of the Concertina

The Concertina consists of three major parts, mounted in wooden, or wood and metal ends: the bellows, the action (buttons, levers and pads) and the reeds.

The bellows may be quite stiff when the instrument is new, but it is wise to avoid putting too much pressure on them to cause them to stretch. They will become easier after a few weeks of normal playing. Never force the bellows open or closed without pressing a button (the air release button is provided if you need to open or close the bellows without actually sounding a note; this is likely to happen frequently on the Anglo model). Take care not to stretch the bellows too far; the corners of the bellows could otherwise become slack or damaged, and the screws fixing the bellows to the ends could loosen, causing leakage.

To inspect or service the action or reeds, the ends have to be removed from the bellows. This is done by removing the screws on each side of each end, six, eight or twelve, depending on how many sides the instrument has. On the Hohner concertina, the reeds are mounted on a separate wooden plate, lodged in the bellows and easily lifted out. The reeds in both cases are grouped in pairs, each pair being controlled by a button. On the English concertina the pairs make the same note; on the Anglo they make different ones. If a reed does not sound, the reason may be that it is impeded by a small foreign body which can easily be removed. If a reed goes badly out of tune, it should be replaced or tuned by an expert. Service for Hohner concertinas is available from your Hohner dealer. For service for older concertinas, there are a number of tuners and repairers who advertise in the folk music press.

The most sensitive part of the instrument is the action. To expose the action of a Hohner concertina, remove the end as described above. On the inside, near the reeds, are two small steel screws; when these are removed, the whole assembly of reeds and action will lift out. With a traditional concertina, the end usually has to be split to expose the action. There are usually two long thin screws, one in the centre of the little finger slide, and one in the centre of the thumb strap mounting on an English, one near the wrist strap bar and one near the buttons on an Anglo. The usual reasons for failure of the action are a broken spring or a loose pad; either of these would result in the note continuing to sound when the button is no longer being pressed. In the case of a broken spring, the button would also stay down. A quick look at the other springs will show how they are mounted. A loose pad is easily re-glued; check that the pad fits snugly over the hole when in position. A small touch of sewing machine oil can be applied to the pivots of the action if necessary, but care must be taken that there is not enough excess to allow any to be sucked into the reeds when playing.

Care of the concertina is generally common sense, and the amount and frequency of maintenance needed are usually directly proportional to the force with which the instrument is played. A musician for a Morris or other ritual dance side, who plays forcefully out in the open air most of the time may find that his reeds need attention more often. A brass reed goes out of tune more quickly than a steel reed, a point to take into consideration when choosing an older instrument.

Early maintenance is best. For this reason it is wise to act quickly if a reed is going out of tune; it can then be re-tuned without being weakened. As you become familiar with the feel of the action, a button with less than the usual resistance will give you an early warning that the spring on that lever is getting weak.

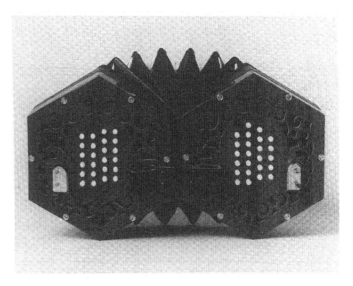

Where To Go From Here

Now the real process of becoming a concertina player begins. Work out your own tunes and song accompaniments by ear or from music. Any book of songs with guitar chords can be used for a start towards working out accompaniments, and for those familiar with them, many written piano accompaniments can be adapted to the concertina. For dance tunes, the standard collections usually print a melody line only. The more familiar you become with the fingering pattern of the instrument, the easier it will be to work things out by ear.

If you meet a key which you have not played in before, (many fiddle tunes are written in A, and convenient singing keys vary greatly from person to person), it may be an idea to familiarise yourself with it by playing scales first. Find the note which starts the key on the fingering chart and work up or down in the standard sequence. The number of sharps or flats at the beginning of each line (the 'key signature') will tell you the number of times you will have to use rows 3 or 1x in a scale.

Printed